SUPER
CHAMPIONS
OF AUTO RACING

Rick Mears on the track at Indianapolis.

Penske

SUPER CHAMPIONS OF AUTO RACING

ROSS R. OLNEY

Illustrated with photographs

CLARION BOOKS

TICKNOR & FIELDS: A HOUGHTON MIFFLIN COMPANY

NEW YORK

TO MY GRANDSONS,
R.J. AND CHRISTOPHER

CLARION BOOKS
Ticknor & Fields, a Houghton Mifflin Company
Copyright © 1984 by Ross R. Olney

Printed in the U.S.A.

LIBRARY OF CONGRESS CATALOGING IN PUBLICATION DATA
Olney, Ross Robert, 1929–
    Super-champions of auto racing.

    Includes index.

    Summary: Profiles six contemporary racing super-
champions and describes various types of professional
automobile racing such as championship, NASCAR, sprint,
and drag racing.

    1. Automobile racing drivers—Biography—Juvenile
literature.   2. Automobile racing—Juvenile literature.
[1. Automobile racing drivers.   2. Automobile racing]
I.Title.
GV1032.A10444   1984   796.7′2′0922 [B]   83-14407
RNF ISBN 0-89919-259-9
PAP ISBN 0-89919-289-0

RNFX & PAPX 10 9 8 7 6 5 4 3 2 1

ACKNOWLEDGMENTS

The author would like to thank the following for photos, advice, information, and for the continuing support;

Pete Biro, Long Beach Grand Prix Association
Al Bloemker, Indianapolis Motor Speedway
Chan Bush, photographer
Kenny Cason, Chief Auto Parts
Herb Dodge, photographer
Ben Foote, Agajanian Enterprises
Steve Forsythe, Caesars Palace
Deke Houlgate, Pennzoil
Hank Ives, Los Angeles Times
Bob Russo, Riverside International Raceway
Bill Wishon, darkroom technician

All photographs are by Ross R. Olney except for the following, which are used through the courtesy of: Bridgestone Tires, 102; Caesars Palace, 112; Chan Bush, 49; Gould Inc., 3, 80, 91, 94; Herb Dodge, 77; National Hot Rod Association, 55; Pennzoil, 84, 88; Sears, Roebuck and Co., 68.

CONTENTS

INTRODUCTION

Auto racing is one of the most exciting sports of all. It is also one of the most popular sports of all. Did you know that more people throughout the world watch auto racing than any other sport but soccer? Can you guess which sports event attracts the single largest audience in the United States?

The baseball World Series?

The football Superbowl?

A great tennis or golf match?

No, it's not any of these. It is the 500-mile auto race at the Indianapolis Motor Speedway in Indiana every Memorial Day weekend.

More than 400,000 people attend the race in person. Of course many, many millions more watch it on TV or listen to it on the radio. It is a wild, circuslike, exciting "happening" in mid-America each spring.

Indianapolis-type racing, known as Indy or Championship car racing, is only one class of auto racing. One of the greatest drivers of all is an Indy car racer. He is fairly new to the sport, too. He is Rick Mears. There are many, many classes in the sport.

Stock car racing, especially NASCAR racing, draws great crowds of people. NASCAR stands for National Association for Stock Car Auto Racing. These races among roaring big stock cars almost always finish with the cars wheel-to-wheel. Stock cars look just like the cars on the street. But under the hood they are nothing at all like them. They are cars that have been adapted for speed. And they are pure excitement on a racetrack.

One of the best NASCAR drivers, a NASCAR champion, is Darrell Waltrip. Both Mears and Waltrip are national champions in their class of racing. This means they have won more than anybody else.

Racing on dirt tracks or in backwoods country is one of the most exciting of all forms of racing.

This is an Indy car, the "Gould Charge" of champion Rick Mears.

This wild and woolly sport is known as off-road racing. Usually it takes place far out in the desert. But sometimes off-road races are run on a course at a regular speedway like Riverside International Raceway in California. One of the best off-road racers in the sport is Roger Mears, Rick Mears' older brother.

Sprint and midget car racing is very dangerous. These cars are open-wheel, open-cockpit cars that race very close to each other on small, oval, quarter-mile and half-mile dirt tracks. Spins and flips seem to happen more often than in any other type of racing. Ron Shuman is one of the best at sprint and midget driving. He wins often, and he is always a threat to win.

Drag racing is different but just as exciting. In this type of racing, cars rush away from a starting line to see who can get to the end of a quarter-mile track first. They do this in different classes of cars. One of the favorite classes of the fans is the Funny Car class. One of the best Funny Car drivers of all is Billy Meyer.

Many fans feel that Formula 1 Grand Prix racing is the top class. These drivers, cars, and teams travel around the world racing on "road courses"

This Funny Car is driven by Billy Meyer, one of the best in drag racing.

with left and right turns and faster and slower sections. They race in many different countries. From this type of racing comes a world champion. Alan Jones won the world championship in 1980.

There are many other types of racing. In SCCA (Sports Car Club of America) there are dozens of different classes, for different types of cars. Some of these groups are amateur classes. These are classes of racing where the drivers race for fun and trophies, but not for money. Here racing is a hobby, just for the thrill of the challenge.

Why do so many people come to watch car races at Indy or a NASCAR track? Why do they come to watch races between sprint cars on a dirt track? Or a drag race? Or a wild off-road race where the cars bounce and fly through the air?

Do they attend to see crashes? There are almost always crashes at a motor race. So they want to see a driver get hurt? Or worse?

Perhaps a few people attend for these reasons. But almost all of those who come to see auto races do so for a different reason. They attend to see men and women challenge danger and get away with it. They want to see two cars racing

Off-road racing is wild and dangerous. These two off-roaders are sailing over a bump in their fight for the lead — and over the photographer as well.

beside each other in a very dangerous way—and *not* crash. They want to see drivers move along the fine line of disaster and come through without harm.

If you have ever been to an auto race where a

driver has been hurt, you know. The fun is gone then. Many people just go home. There's no thrill in seeing somebody lose. This driver has lost the gamble, so there is no more challenge. There is no more excitement. When the race resumes, it is much less fun.

In this book you will read about the top drivers in some of the top classes of racing. These are the races where a lot of money can be won. Some of these drivers are millionaires. Most will be eventually, if they survive.

They earn their money though. Any type of racing, on any track, can be deadly. All motor racing drivers put their lives on the line, even when no prize money is being paid. For the drivers in this book, riches make the victories even sweeter.

Roger Mears

ONE

ROGER MEARS

Off-road racing is dangerous and very hard on car and driver. It is one of the most demanding of all motor sports. It is also very enjoyable, according to most of the drivers.

From motorcycles to big trucks, there are many classes. Some racers are built especially for off-road racing. Others are changed from street cars to off-road racers by mechanics and people who are skilled in rebuilding cars.

The racers bounce and jump about. They roar along straight parts of the course. Then they leap over gulleys and ditches, slamming down *hard* on the other side. They skid and slide and throw huge clouds of dust behind. Soon they are caked with mud and dust, but they roar on.

Many of the cars don't finish the race. The

course is just too tough. After every race, officials go out to look for the cars that have broken down. Finding all of them can take some time. Some off-road races are hundreds of miles long. They sometimes wind through rocky, wild backcountry with no houses or service stations for many miles.

Roger Mears is one of the very best of the off-road racers. He and his younger brother, Rick, raced off-road almost before they did anything else in racing. Rick went on to other types of racing, and Roger did, too, but he also continued to race off-road.

Roger Mears stayed with off-road, not only because he is the top champion in that type of racing — he loves it. "Indy car racing has such a fine line in driving style," he said recently. "You can't make any mistakes in an Indy car. That's probably why I like to jump into trucks and go off-road racing."

A good example of Mears' skill with these bucking bronco cars is a recent race at Riverside International Raceway in California. Normally this is a paved-road course, but once each year it's different. Promoters use bulldozers to carve out a rugged dirt course that winds in and around the paved course. They cut deep gulleys and build sharp hills and lay telephone poles directly across the track. They do everything they can to make the track look just like wild desert and mountain country.

They call the race the Bridgestone Off-Road Race (it is sponsored by Bridgestone Tires) and hold a series of events. There are six races throughout the day for various types of cars and trucks. In 1982 Mears was in three of the six races. He drove a pickup truck racer in one, a two-seater racer in another, and a dune-buggy-type racer in the third.

He won the first race. And the second. And the third.

Roger Mears was the racing star of the day. He spent almost as much time on the victory stand collecting trophies and prize money as he did on the course racing. On the victory stand after the third win he tried to squirt some champagne at the photographers. But the day was very hot and the champagne had gone flat. It barely trickled out of the bottle. "That's about how I feel right now," said the tired champion with a broad grin.

Many off-road drivers also try Indy-type racing

Mears drives all types of off-road cars. Here he is in a single-seater dune-buggy-type car.

because the prizes are so big, and so did Mears. As time passed, he became better and better at this type of racing, too. But at first his luck wasn't very good. Mears was driving at an Indy car race in Cleveland, Ohio, in 1982. He was at the wheel of the sleek Machinists' Union Penske racer, speeding along smoothly, battling for a better position.

Ahead, driver Dick Simon lost a part on his

car. It was a half-shaft, a short steel tube that connects the rear wheel to the transmission. Before anybody could get the half-shaft off the track, along came Roger Mears at top speed.

Mears might as well have been deep in the Mexican desert with rocks flying about, where this type of accident usually happens. Simon's half-shaft bounced up and broke off a part of Mears' rear brake system. Now Mears had no brakes on his speeding racer.

Then a part of the same half-shaft jammed the throttle on Mears' race car. He had no rear brakes. With his throttle jammed open, he couldn't slow down!

He tried tapping the front brakes, but he had a good idea of what might happen. And it did. Instantly the car began to spin. Then it crashed into the wall very hard. In fact, it broke down part of the wall. It also ripped out a TV camera that had been covering the race for people around the United States. All they saw was the car coming; then their screens went blank.

Mears was rushed to the hospital with a concussion. But he recovered and returned to racing soon. And he was as good as ever, especially off-road. Mears enjoys racing both on closed courses like Riverside or out in open desert.

"Desert events are fun for the competitors and the teams," Mears explained, "but the closed courses are super for the fans, who can see all the action. Besides, I like the stand-on-the-gas type of racing. In desert events you go as fast as you can, but it still is a pacesetting situation. Your first thought is to finish. On closed courses, you go as fast as you can without tipping the truck over, and I love it. In desert racing, you have to do a lot of reading of markers to find the fast way

Roger Mears is a champion in off-road trucks.

through the open terrain. On the short course, you just learn the course and *go*."

Roger Mears is the older brother of Rick, who is best known now as an Indy car driver. The two brothers are close. They often race together in the same race when Roger is racing in Indy cars or Rick in off-road cars. They grew up doing the same things together, as brothers often do. They became winners in off-road races together. They became known as "the Mears Gang" around off-road courses.

Roger Mears has always been known for his uncanny ability to drive on rugged trails at top speed. He seems to know exactly when to slow and when to press down on the gas. He can make his cars last, a valuable asset in off-road racing. He won the major race at Riverside in 1974, 1975, 1977, 1982, and 1983, and in 1978 he won the famous Parker 400 off-road race. This is a grueling 400-mile race through the terrible heat of the desert. He has won many, many other off-road races.

Riverside is the "home track" for the Mears gang, who live in Bakersfield, California. Reporters recently asked who had won more professional races at Riverside than anybody else. Most of the top driving stars have raced there over the years. Many, such as A. J. Foyt, Richard Petty, Gordon Johncock, Darrell Waltrip, Cale Yarborough, Mario Andretti, and others have driven in dozens of races there. Was it one of these great stars? Or could it have been former road-racing star Dan Gurney?

Roger Mears is the champ. By 1983 he had won *eighteen* major events at the California track, far more than anybody else.

Besides off-road racing and Indy cars, Roger Mears has raced in most of the other professional

A cool victory-stand drink for Roger Mears after a hard-fought race.

racing cars — stock cars, sprint cars, ministocks, midgets, and Super-Vee racers.

He is making a bigger and bigger name for himself in Indy-type racing, though his first year at the Indianapolis Speedway was not so pleasant.

The year was 1982, Mears' first year at the Brickyard (so-called because long ago the track was paved with bricks). He was starting the race from far back in the field. This is not unusual for a first-timer at Indy. Usually the veterans qualify fast enough to be up front for the start. But Roger Mears had a good car and he felt he could do well in the race.

He also felt good that his kid brother, a former winner at Indy, was up front, on the pole. Roger Mears knew that the Mears brothers had a good chance that day. He knew that *he* had a good chance.

But there was an accident as the thirty-three race cars roared down the main stretch for the start of the big race. Some cars began to spin. Roger Mears managed to get out of the way and miss them. But then another car came roaring up from the rear. That driver couldn't get stopped.

He slammed into the back of Mears' car. The Mears car was too badly damaged to continue in the race.

Mears was unhappy but not discouraged. He knew that it was just "racing luck." Still, in his first 500-mile race at Indy he hadn't even managed to get across the starting line on the first lap.

He has done much better in other Indy-type races. In 1983 Roger Mears became one of the regular racers to finish high in the field. Although he hasn't *won* an Indy-type race yet, experts say it is only a matter of time.

Roger Mears is also known as one of the most versatile drivers in big-time racing. It seems he can win in almost any type of car. He won the famous Pikes Peak Hill Climb in 1972 and 1973. This is a wild dash up the side of the well-known mountain in Colorado. "I'll always remember my first Pikes Peak win," says Mears. He calls it one of his favorite victories of all.

When the brothers are asked about each other, they both say the same thing. Each is talented, but the other is an even better driver. Each is a winner in whatever type of racing he chooses. Roger Mears tried to explain his relationship with Rick. "My brother and I both wanted the

Roger Mears waits impatiently while his crew adds fuel and checks tires on his Indy car.

same things. We said, 'There are two ways to get there, to have a rich sponsor, or work our way up.' When we began working our way up, we either had to start in sprint cars or try to work in the formula and Indy-type cars. Rick chose the formula-type cars and I chose the sprints. I went my way and he went his."

And now the brothers are racing against each other in different types of racing. Each has become wealthy. At off-road races, Roger Mears is the top champion. Fans crowd around him, demand his autograph, and try to touch his car. He has remained warm and friendly to them. He always seems to have time to stop and talk or to sign an autograph or pose for a picture. Although he has reached the top of his field, he has not become bigheaded.

The Mears family has always been in racing. Bill Mears, the father, started racing jalopies, old stock cars, when he was a teen-ager in Kansas. He was following the lead of two uncles who also raced. Mears drove in Kansas, Texas, and Oklahoma, winning the Kansas state championship in 1948. Bill Mears was a man with auto racing in his blood. When he married, his wife, Skip, followed him from track to track. So did their two sons, Roger and Rick, and their daughter, Robin, when they came along.

Roger Mears started racing go-karts when he was twelve years old. Rick was seven, and soon he followed in his older brother's footsteps. It wasn't long before both boys were beating everybody else in whatever they raced, so more and more often they were racing each other for the big prize. This bothered their father. One night the two boys were far ahead of everybody else in a

100-mile race. They were wheel to wheel, battling each other for the lead in the sprint-buggy race. A sprint buggy is a car like a dune buggy.

Bill Mears became so agitated and angry and worried that the two of them would crash into each other that he rushed to the edge of the track. Each time they would roar by, he would throw huge clods of dirt at them. The crowd loved it.

"Wait until the last few laps, when it counts," he taught the boys. After all, he pointed out, they had already beaten everybody else. "Why go full-bore the whole time and tear up the cars?" he demanded.

Skip Mears insists that both Roger and Rick are equally skilled in racing cars. And both are highly competitive, she points out. "But they are close," she says, "and they care about each other." She admits that when they race each other, it is hard for her to handle. "There is no way of watching both at the same time. I send up double prayers and hope for the best for both of them."

The brothers were close even as children. Skip Mears recollected the time Roger was fifteen and had a job as a busboy at a Chinese restaurant. He was saving his money and hiding it. "One day we passed a bicycle shop, and Rick saw these shiny new ten-speeds and was wishing he could have one. We couldn't afford it. But Roger went home and got out his money and bought a bike for Rick."

Robin, who is twelve years younger than Roger, raced a few times to fill out the Mears family legend. She now watches both of her famous brothers race. The family is close-knit. They work together in Bill Mears' excavating

Roger Mears (center) and his brother Rick chat with car owner Roger Penske (left) in the garage at Ontario Motor Speedway.

business when they are not away racing. They play together as a group. The boys are now involved in flying ultralight airplanes around Bakersfield.

Racing has not always been kind to Roger Mears. Injury is a risk in racing, and Roger Mears has had his share of it. In 1980 he took the midget owned by the family to Ascot Speedway in Los Angeles for a race. The car was called the Mears Gang Guinn Special. It was a fast little open-wheel, open-cockpit race car, and with it Mears expected to win.

But something went wrong. Sliding high, Mears was bumped by another car. The Mears midget went end over end four times down the track. Inside, an unconscious Mears jerked and slammed about like a rag doll. Both his arms were broken.

In his hospital bed, Roger Mears grinned. He was anxious to get well and get back to racing. Of his car he said, "It's got all the best and latest safety equipment. It saved me. The arm restraints keep an unconscious driver from letting his arms out. Mine were in. They were injured because I was hanging on to the steering wheel so hard when it happened. If it weren't for the safety restraints, I probably wouldn't have any arms left."

Soon Roger Mears was back racing with the top stars in both Indy-type and off-road racing. He never quits. He drove the tough Baja 1000 with a broken arm. This is a race over the ruggedest possible Mexican terrain. It goes the length of Baja California from top to bottom, for 1,000 cruel and punishing miles. Mears had instructed his doctor to make a special cast for his arm for the race. Despite being slammed about in the car and in constant, severe pain, he drove on.

What do the famous brothers think when they are on the track against each other? Rick spoke for both of them. "I realize he's my brother when I see him on the track, and as long as I'm outrunning him, I'm a little careful with him. But if he's outrunning me," he continued with a chuckle, "I'll work a little harder against him. There's nobody I would rather beat than my older brother, but there's nobody I'd rather be beaten by than my older brother, so it works both ways."

Roger Mears was in Bakersfield when Rick won the Indy 500 in 1979. Back at Indy they were dousing Rick with champagne. In Bakersfield, a gang of pals doused Roger Mears with beer in a wild celebration. Roger was happy and laughing and proud of his kid brother. "I was so happy for Rick, the beer and my tears kind of ran together. The beer kind of covered up my crying."

While Roger Mears continues his domination of off-road racing, he is trying for the greater glory and money of Indy-type racing. "What I really want is to drive Champ cars [Indy racers]," he says. And he has been doing just that, racing on what is called "the Championship Trail." This is a series of Indy-car races for CART (Championship Auto Racing Teams), the same series his brother races in. Roger Mears has earned rides in some of the best cars on the circuit because of his talent for racing and finishing. He has been finishing higher and higher in the fields, and he often beats his brother.

Many fans have seen the brother act finish one-two in off-road racing several times. One time it might be Roger in front, the next time Rick. What everybody is now waiting for is a one-two at Indy.

It's hard to predict who'll be number one and who'll be number two.

Ron Shuman

T W O

RON SHUMAN

Many racing fans think that sprint car and midget car racing is best of all. They think that this is racing at its wildest and most exciting. They think the drivers fight hardest to win and take the biggest chances.

They could be right.

Sprint cars and midgets are where many of today's top racing stars got their start. A. J. Foyt was a sprint car and midget car driver. So were Pancho Carter, Gary Bettenhausen, Roger Mears, Mike Mosley, Mario Andretti and Mel Kenyon. So was the great Parnelli Jones.

Today's top star in sprints and midgets is good-looking, hard-driving Ron Shuman. Shuman drives like a man who *must* win. Of course he doesn't always win. Sometimes he crashes and sometimes his car breaks down. But when Ron Shuman starts a race you feel he has a good chance of winning. He drives to win in spite of the possibility of breakdowns and dangerous crashes. And he has become a crowd favorite, very popular with racing fans.

A sprint car is an open-cockpit, open-wheel racer that looks, according to many fans, the way a race car *should* look. It looks old-fashioned in a day when most racing cars look like something from outer space. A midget is a smaller version of a sprint car. Sprint cars race sprint cars and midgets race midgets. During a race these cars often bounce into end-over-end crashes. When two of them get close, their wheels might touch. Then one or the other — or both — will go flying through the air.

The races are usually run on oval-shaped dirt tracks. Sometimes a midget or a sprint car gets its wheel caught in a groove in the track. Then the car flips and bounces. Sometimes drivers are seriously hurt — or worse.

None of these risks seem to bother Ron Shuman. He drives as fast as possible all the time.

Shuman always knew he wanted to be a racer.

From his younger days in Arizona, he dreamed of being a racing driver. He was fifteen when he and his older brother, Billy, began to race motorcycles. Both became winners in area races. Shuman's brother began racing modified stock cars on quarter-mile tracks, and Ron followed soon after.

"I was always a step behind him," says Shuman. Billy went into sprint car racing and finally U.S. Auto Club (USAC) sprint cars on the traveling circuit. Shuman's father encouraged his sons in their racing, and soon young Ron was also traveling and racing sprint cars. He was realizing his dream. Eventually Billy decided to race locally and not on the national circuit. Ron kept right on traveling.

Now in his late twenties, Ron Shuman travels on the sprint and midget car circuits nine months each year. He is doing what he wants to do with his life. "I have a mechanic and a helper who travels with the car. I go in the motor home with my wife and four-year-old son. We meet at the track and race, then we head for the next race. You gotta really want to do it."

Of course, like every other young driver on the

circuit, Shuman has his eye on the Indianapolis Speedway. Though he is a winner, it takes more than winning to race at Indy. There was a time when a young driver worked his way up through the dangerous sprints and midgets and then was hired to drive at Indy. This was the way it worked for many of the top drivers of the past. They had "paid their dues."

But the Speedway has changed, and Shuman knows it. He knows that a driver now must bring a huge sponsorship with him to a car owner. He must already have signed up somebody with millions of dollars. Talent isn't enough, and it isn't even the most important thing anymore. Still, sprint car drivers can earn a pretty good income. One recent week, Shuman drove in three races in three different states. He won all three. His total prize money was over $21,000. Not a bad week's wages.

"If it was just racing ability, I'd be there [at Indy] now," Shuman says without bitterness. "If I went there now, it would be because somebody bought my way, and not because of my talent, and that would hurt the self-satisfaction. You don't get a ride on pure talent, and if you do it isn't much of a car."

Mario Andretti, a world champion in Formula 1 cars like this, started his career in sprint and midget racers. Like Shuman, he had very little money but exceptional talent.

Shuman will look anybody in the eye and admit that in his earlier days he was a problem for the police of his town. He even goaded them into chasing him. He was heading for real trouble and then he began racing cars on weekends. Racing, he feels, turned his life around. It kept him busy on weekends. He applied himself to racing. It was a sport that thrilled him, and he didn't need other kicks to enjoy life.

These days, when he has the time, he goes to schools, shows movies of racing, and talks to young students about his career. The point of his lectures is *safety:* how to ride a bicycle safely and, eventually, how to drive a car safely. Shuman enjoys these talks. He knows that in his earlier life he needed help. He considers that he was one of the "bad guys" as a youth. His first night away from home and parents, at age fourteen, was spent in a facility for problem boys. He owes his change of attitude to the sport of racing. That is why he spends time now talking to students.

Meanwhile, he keeps racing, and that is how he wound up at Ascot Speedway in Los Angeles in 1981. But it was not an ordinary midget race. This was the famous Turkey Night Grand Prix, a major race sponsored by Valvoline, a major company. It is an annual race promoted by the well-known J. C. Agajanian, a prominent name in racing. It is *the* midget race of the year.

Every top midget car driver — men and women who also generally drive sprint cars — was there. They came from all over the country and from other countries to drive in the Turkey Night Grand Prix. Almost every Indy winner had at some time in the past taken part in it. The grandstands were jammed with fans in a festive mood, waiting for the forty-first annual Turkey Night race to begin.

For the previous two years the race had been won by the same driver, Ron Shuman. Nobody had ever won it three years in a row. The only other driver to come close had been A. J. Foyt. But Shuman was there with a good car. He planned to try as hard as he could. Of course the odds were against him. How could anybody win such a race three times? It didn't seem possible. It was difficult enough even to *finish* the Turkey Night race.

That thought wasn't stopping Ron Shuman. He just grinned. "I don't win a lot," he said mod-

Midget racers tend to bounce and flip. Here Ron Shuman goes through a *wild* ride, but he wasn't injured.

estly, "but I seem to win the big ones." Then he donned his fireproof driver's uniform and attached the arm restraints to keep his arms down in case the car flipped. Finally he pulled on the heavy crash helmet.

From the infield, his wife and young son watched. They love the racing life, though it is a dangerous, restless one. They love the crowds and the roar of the engines, and they love the cheers for Shuman, especially when he is winning.

Down in the pit section, crews began shoving cars out onto the track. The drivers strolled alongside. Then, with the cars lined up in starting positions, drivers crawled into the little cockpits. Ron Shuman's car was in fifth place in a field of thirty cars. The drivers were introduced, and each was then secured in the cockpit with heavy safety belts. Finally, a fleet of wreckers and other push cars pulled into position behind each of the midgets. The little racers have no starter and must be pushed to get their engines started. One by one they started and buzzed away as the push cars dropped back into the infield.

Soon everybody was in starting order, circling

the track slowly in a group, engines sounding angry and ready. Around the oval track they went, picking up speed. As they snarled out of the fourth turn, each driver watched the starter. The green flag snapped up as the starter waved it wildly. Every driver stabbed down on his gas pedal and the angry buzz turned to a roar. As one single group, the field of cars shot ahead into the first turn.

Midgets and sprints handle much alike on a dirt track. They thunder down the short straightaway and then the driver flips the front wheels hard over to the left, then back to the right. This throws the car into a long, four-wheel drift, or slide. All the way around the turn they slide, side by side and almost touching. Their engines race in bursts to keep the controlled slide going. This is the quickest way around the turns on a short dirt track. In groups they slide, with each driver fighting to maintain control and not bump anybody else.

It is *thrilling* racing to watch — according to some, the most thrilling of all motor racing.

Shuman, a master of the speeding midgets, fought his way toward the front of the pack.

Every eye in the grandstands was on him. But his car was giving him problems. It wasn't handling right. There is no time for a pit stop in a midget race. You go all out to win, all the way, with time for nothing but racing.

Many of the drivers were still thinking about the problems in an earlier race that night. The car of former midget champion Mel Kenyon had been bumped by another car. Kenyon's car spun away and flipped upside down. So had the cars of Eddie Leavitt and Chunky Koster. Although the drivers were not seriously hurt, all three cars were out of the race because of the spectacular crash.

But that race had been a warm-up race. This was the main event! Again there was trouble on the track. Shuman saw it happening. Ken Nichols' car flipped over and bounced wildly, the driver flopping about in the cockpit. Other cars darted right and left to miss Nichols. But Bob Davison couldn't get out of the way. He flipped over and bounded end over end. Three other cars skidded into the wall to avoid the bouncing racers. All in all, five cars were out of the race in the wild crash.

The red flag was waved and the race stopped. There were too many wrecked cars on the track to continue. They had to be removed. But this delay gave Ron Shuman the time he needed to work on his car. When the race started again, the car was working better than before.

Shuman knew that he had a chance to win the race. His car was running more smoothly and he felt good. The other racers fought him as he slid through turn after turn. Big clods of dirt flew from under his spinning rear wheels and plastered the walls all the way around the turns. Before the race the walls were clean, with black and white stripes for visibility. By then they were mud caked and dark.

Ahead, Buster Venard's speeding midget moved too low in a turn. His wheels bit the inside berm of the track. Instantly the car was flipping end over end. Venard's car bounced *seven times* in the terrible crash. The driver climbed out, shaken but unhurt.

Shuman drove on, trying as hard as he could to move up closer and closer to the leader. This race was one of the most important ones of the season, and he smelled a possible victory. As a two-time

Turkey Night winner, he knew the crowd was watching him. He could see them waving him on, but he couldn't hear their cheers over the sound of his own roaring engine.

The crowd hoped to see him win. They would love to see a three-time winner, to see history made at Ascot. On roared the little racing cars.

Then Jack Hawley's car drifted too far out on a turn and hit the infamous Ascot "cushion." This condition exists on many dirt tracks where dirt clods have been thrown up high in the turns as the cars slide around. Soon there is a soft cushion of loose dirt high on the track.

The Hawley midget caught the cushion and flipped into the wall. The other cars slowed as rescue workers helped Hawley run clear of the crash.

The race was becoming a war, with mounting casualties! Still Shuman drove on. He was cool and careful down the straightaways and in the corners. His car still wasn't right, but it was better than before. He was drawing closer and closer to the front. He knew his chances for a win were still good.

Suddenly two more cars were bouncing down

the track. Steve Kinser had touched Bob Ellis and both cars were out of control. When the two cars came to a rest, the red flag came out again. The wreckage had to be cleared. So once again Shuman had time for another quick adjustment. When he came out for the third start of the race, the car was *right*!

He thundered on. You must finish to win, he knew. He wanted to stay out of trouble and finish. He wanted to *win*!

The end of the race was close. Only speedster Jeff Haywood was between Ron Shuman and the lead. Throwing caution to the winds, Shuman went for it. The crowd was in a frenzy. There were only sixteen laps to go on the half-mile track. Shuman made his move. On the eighty-fourth lap, he squeezed past Haywood and into the lead. The crowd thundered approval of the move.

Shuman sailed on, dodging around the backmarkers in the race. These were cars still running but far back in the field. They were being lapped by the leaders.

The Turkey Night race roared on, with Shuman solidly in the lead. His little car was humming smoothly. If nobody made a mistake or spun in front of him, he knew he could win. If his car held together, he would win. Only then did he notice that his engine was showing no oil pressure at all. His engine could stop at any instant, but he drove on.

The checkered flag was raised high by the starter and snapped down as Shuman sped down the short main stretch of the track. The crowd roared.

He'd *won*!

Shuman was the first ever to win the famous Thanksgiving Day race at Ascot three times. But Ron Shuman is perhaps the top midget car driver in the country, and the top sprint car driver, too. He won the sprint car Triple Crown in 1981. That means he won the U.S. Nationals in Iowa, the Ascot Pacific Coast Nationals in California, and the Western World Championship in Arizona all in the same year. These are the three most important sprint car races of the year. Shuman has won one or another of these races in other years as well.

Indy? Shuman has raced there, too. But not at the *big* track. At Indianapolis there is the famed two-and-one-half mile track where they have one

Ron Shuman is also a champion in sprint cars. He is shown driving one here.

race each year. Then there is another famous track, a dirt track, at the fairgrounds in Indianapolis. This is where they have some of the major sprint car races in the Midwest. One very important one for sprint cars is the race the night before the Indianapolis Speedway race across town.

Shuman was there in 1982 to drive in a car he had never seen before. The car-owner had hired him by telephone. In the grandstands were thousands of people who were there to see the 500-mile race the next day. These people also loved sprint car racing.

Shuman won the race.

After a race, the Shumans move on. They travel from track to track, from race to race. In any car, on any track, he is the favorite to win. He will give it all he has. He is a natural-born race car driver who loves what he is doing. He has nerves of ice and no fear at all of the bouncing, flipping midgets and sprints. He drives to win.

"I've never been really hurt in a crash," he says. But Shuman knows that he must soon consider a change in his dramatic life-style. His son will begin school in another year. Then Shuman can no longer travel with his family. Perhaps he will concentrate on racing in Arizona and California. Perhaps by then he will have found a sponsor and be racing on the Championship Trail, in Indy cars.

Or maybe he will still be the most consistent winner in midgets and sprints.

Proof? Shuman came back to Ascot in 1982 and once again won the biggest midget race of all, the Turkey Night Grand Prix. Very likely no driver will *ever* equal this record of wins. If he wins it one more time, he says, he will retire from that particular race. "It wouldn't be any fun *not* to win anymore," he explains. Though Ron Shuman makes a good living, he races because he loves to race.

Ron Shuman in a competitive Indy car at the famous speedway would be something to see. He has waited a long time. He has polished his skills in racing. He is fearless.

Maybe next year.

Billy Meyer

THREE

BILLY MEYER

"Funny Cars" are funny cars indeed. And they are driven by some of the most daring drivers in all of drag racing. Billy Meyer is a Funny Car driver, one of the youngest and one of the best.

Meyer, a thirty-year-old Texan, was a champion in amateur go-karts. Then, instead of moving slowly up through the ranks in other classes of racing, he jumped directly into professional competition in drag racing — in Funny Cars. That is how Billy Meyer runs his life. He makes decisions and then he acts upon them.

A Funny Car is a low, sleek, very fast dragster. It has a shell of a body that looks something like a standard passenger car. The engine is in front. The driver sits where the backseat used to be. Funny Cars are nothing at all like passenger cars.

They are race cars that only *look* a little like passenger cars.

Funny Cars race in pairs, like all the other cars in drag racing. Two by two the cars line up, side by side. Carefully the drivers edge the cars forward to the starting line. They watch the "Christmas tree" starting lights to tell them when they are close to the line. When they are exactly on the line, two small lights atop the tree are lit.

Then the larger yellow lights blink down the sides of the tree, one by one for each of the two lanes.

Finally, green lights snap on for each lane.

Instantly, both cars rocket away in a great blast of noise and power.

The idea is to get to the other end of the drag strip first. That's one quarter mile away — one thousand three hundred and twenty feet. Lights flicker next to the lane of the winner at the far end of the strip. This is to tell the officials at the starting line who won. All the timing is done electronically. Sometimes the difference between the two cars cannot be measured by the naked eye, so fast is each and so close are the races.

Although he began as one of the youngest,

Billy Meyer at speed in one of his famous Funny Cars.

Meyer soon became one of the best at this dangerous game. He was the youngest driver ever to earn a pro Funny Car license in 1970 (at age sixteen). He was the youngest driver to win a national Funny Car race (twenty years old). He was the youngest Funny Car driver to hold a national speed record (twenty years old). At that age, Meyer lowered the record to 6.19 seconds for a quarter mile during the U.S. Nationals.

None of these feats were easy for Meyer. Early in his career he suffered two serious accidents on the drag strip. Both times his expensive Funny Car was destroyed. In one of the crashes he broke his collarbone, punctured a lung, and had a concussion. In the other accident he burned his hands badly. In the first accident, his parachute failed. Funny Cars use a parachute to help them stop at the end of the strip after a high speed run. Otherwise brakes would simply burn out.

With no parachute, the car shot off the end of the strip. Then it plunged into a deep pond. Meyer was lucky to escape with his life, thanks in part to mechanic Ronnie Guyman, who pulled him out.

Still, Billy Meyer continued his fight to the top of the sport of Funny Car racing.

Then he suddenly changed his direction. He decided to go for the world land speed record. This meant driving a different type of car, on a different track, with different people, and required completely different knowledge. But Meyer had made a decision.

"It doesn't matter how much I like something," he explained. "If it starts failing or losing money, I look elsewhere. I can do anything. I have a good background. I've done selling, I've owned real estate. I was fortunate to be raised in an atmosphere of positive thinking and goal setting. These are things we can all use. I set goals and I try to meet them."

Meyer's father is president of Success Motivation Institute. Meyer was raised to believe he can do whatever he sets his mind to doing.

And if he fails? "If I don't meet my goals, I turn around and look at the alternatives. I don't mean to sound negative, but I like to do things at such an extreme that I can't do them just for the fun of it."

The land speed record attempt fizzled. There were problems with the sponsors and with finances that positive thinking could not cure. Billy Meyer was unhappy. He wanted action, and the project was stalled. So after a year Meyer decided to return to drag racing.

And he did it in a *big* way.

To be sure everybody knew he was back, he bought a giant tractor-trailer rig — not a medium-sized one, but a *Texas*-sized rig. Into the trailer he built a complete machine shop. He had stalls for other equipment and for his new Funny Car. And he made room in the trailer for a fully equipped van, to be used as a tow vehicle and crew car.

When the big rig arrived at the first race,

This is the first of Meyer's giant tractor-trailer rigs. His Funny Car is being serviced between elimination heats.

everybody came over to look. It towered over everything. Fans flocked around to see the Meyer crew in action. In drag racing, fans are allowed into the pits next to the cars and drivers and mechanics.

That year, 1977, Billy Meyer placed third in the national standings. Not bad, he thought, for a driver who had just come back to drag racing. Also, he became the youngest driver ever to win an NHRA event. (NHRA is the National Hot Rod Association, the largest and richest of the drag-racing organizations.) Not bad, but it was not good enough either for a goal-setting young man like Billy Meyer.

Besides, 1977 was the year he suffered a serious fire in his car. Tom Blattler, then an NHRA official, described the terrible accident:

"Sometimes a fire in a Funny Car will tunnel back up front, and in the case of the Meyer fire, it exploded the fuel tank. There was an incredible amount of flame, but because of his safety equipment he only suffered burns on his hands.

"The fire quickly burned off the parachute. Meyer was going over 200 miles per hour when the explosion occurred. It finally began to burn the rubber on the tires. It became very difficult to stop.

"You can just try to throw the car into a skid, or into the guardrail. This fire of Meyer's happened at the finish line."

Meyer managed to get stopped in the area beyond the line, but his car was destroyed. Parts of it were scattered along the strip. The body had been blown free and burned and shattered. The experience had been harrowing for the youngest driver in professional Funny Car racing.

But even more amazing, "He won the race," concluded Blattler with a grin. "It was at the finish line that he threw a rod and the fire started."

Billy Meyer is more than just one of the top drivers in the sport. He is unique. Funny Car racing is a sport where the average age of the driver is well over thirty. Usually a few years of drag-racing experience is necessary before a driver becomes a winner. Meyer is the exception.

Age never mattered to Meyer. He pursued his goal of a world championship in Funny Cars. He will doubtless achieve it sooner or later.

"I've driven a Funny Car so many times, it would be hard to describe what it feels like," said

Meyer's hands were burned in this terrible fire. First the fire explodes around the car, then the car body flies off, and finally everything burns. Notice the star on Meyer's helmet in the middle of the fire.

Meyer. "After more than 3,000 runs, it is just like any other job. The same as a golfer having a good drive on the golf course," he added with a grin.

"What keeps it from getting simple is that you have to use your mind during the run." Even though a "run" takes less than six seconds. "I do my own tuning [car preparation] so I must also tune by the seat of my pants on the strip. After you get the races down to inches and all the scientific stuff doesn't work anymore, it's whatever the driver feels, if he is the tuner. And I am, as well as the driver."

After the "scientific stuff" (tire compound, fuel mixture, adhesion factors, and the like) is done, Meyer feels for a slight difference in the clutch, or in the transmission. He looks for a tiny change in fuel consumption. He uses his own instinct when the computers are finished.

Meyer's latest car can go from zero to sixty miles per hour in only *one second*. By the time you say "zero to sixty," he can be going that fast on the drag strip. When he gets to the end of the strip (in less than six seconds) he is usually traveling around *250 miles per hour*. That is quick pickup. That is speed!

Meyer's latest Funny Car is up on its prop between heats. The light plastic body is lowered before the race starts.

In 1981, Billy Meyer agreed to team up with actor Burt Reynolds and director Hal Needham. Both men had long been interested in car racing. Meyer would drive and they would sponsor. As if to prove the deal a good one, Meyer won the very first NHRA Funny Car race of the season. It was the famous Winternationals at Pomona, California. He beat three-time world champion Raymond Beadle and his Blue Max Funny Car in the final race of the day.

Billy Meyer's best time on the quarter-mile drag strip is an amazing 5.89 seconds. This was the track record he set during qualifying for the NHRA Grandnational at Montreal, Canada, in 1981. It is one of the fastest times in all of Funny Car racing.

Meyer's earlier records were for the time elapsed from start to finish of a race (ET). In mid-1982 he set still another one. At the IHRA (International Hot Rod Association) meet in Norwalk, Ohio, he set a world *speed* record. Meyer was going at an astounding 254.23 miles per hour at the end of the quarter-mile strip.

Drag racing in the professional classes is a big-money operation. The cars are worth more than $75,000 and that is only the beginning. Top drivers like Meyer have several sponsors who put a great deal of money into the team. Some of them are in the auto business, and some are not. 7-Eleven Food Stores is a company in the fast-food service business. Yet they are one of the major sponsors of the Meyer/Reynolds/Needham team. The other major sponsor is Chief Auto Parts, a chain of auto supply stores.

Other major teams have sponsors in such fields

as cosmetics, clothing, beverages, and similar non-auto fields.

But the sponsors get their money's worth. For instance Billy Meyer not only wins (and parades the names of his sponsors' products around the country on huge trucks) but he is also a polished public speaker. When Meyer is interviewed, he always works in the names of his sponsors. When he is on TV, the names of his sponsors are always evident. Billy Meyer is a businessman as well as a daredevil race-car driver.

The great blue moving van rumbles into the pits early in the morning. The crew begins to unload. From far over in the grandstands the huge logo of the sponsors can be seen clearly by early arriving fans. By then many other vans and trucks are also arriving and the pits are becoming active. Several major teams have now decided to use moving vans for their operation, so many sponsors' names can be seen.

From the rear of the trailer the crew car is unloaded, then the expensive Funny Car. Everybody has a job to do and every job gets done by the three-man team and extras hired for this race in this town. There are engine men, body men, tuners, "gofers" and other helpers. Meyer himself mixes the fuel and does final tuning of the Funny Car.

Finally, as the sun rises higher and burns off the morning mists, the car is shoved to the staging area. It is time for the first timed qualifying run. By tomorrow, only sixteen Funny Cars will be left of the dozens in the pits. The others will have been eliminated by the timed runs. Only the fastest sixteen qualify to race in the big-money heats the following day. Meyer wants to be one of the sixteen. So he must drive as fast as possible on every run in order to qualify.

Tomorrow the sixteen will compete in four side-by-side runs to determine the overall best. If you win, you go on to the next elimination run. If you lose, you go on to the next racetrack in the next town.

Meyer dons his fireproof driving uniform and crash helmet. After a word with his wife, he snuggles down into the single seat. He is strapped in tightly. Then the raised body of the car is lowered down around him after the engine is started with a roar.

Both cars thunder away from the starting line

in a burst of smoke and speed that stings the nose and hurts the ears. But drag racing fans love it. The cars seem to get smaller and smaller on the track, so fast are they going. Each is straining to get to the end of the strip first. More often than

Billy Meyer is in the "office" before going to work. When the car body is lowered, he will go to the line.

not, Billy Meyer is driving the one that does it.

The crew car shoves the Funny Car back to the pit area. Perhaps the engine will be torn down. The whole car will be checked out very carefully. Then it will be shoved back to the staging area for the next elimination run in an hour or so. Or perhaps, if Meyer has lost, the Funny Car will be loaded into the moving van for the journey to the next track.

Meyer shows neither elation nor sadness in either case. Racing is a business to him, and he is a businessman. The cockpit of his racer is his office. He goes to work, he makes decisions, and his effort is either successful or not. The business is a highly dangerous and very profitable one, but still a business. Billy Meyer views it coolly, like most businessmen. After a race he knows he has done his best, according to his plan, and he has either won or lost. It is time to move on to the next challenge.

"We are representing some outstanding companies and we want to make the best impression possible on the track and off," Meyer explains. "We're all part of one team; me, the crew, the team, and the sponsors."

Billy Meyer is a positive thinking, goal-oriented winner. He will try to win as long as he has decided to try. Then he might look elsewhere. But his decision will be made after looking at all the choices.

You will see Billy Meyer on the drag strip for some time to come, probably. And as long as you do, you will see a young super-champion who is trying his best at every moment to win.

Darrell Waltrip

FOUR

DARRELL WALTRIP

It was the last lap of the Winston 500 race in May, 1982. For 187 laps the huge stock cars had been battling. A few lay smoking on the safety aprons or in the garage. They had been unable to take the strain.

But going into the last lap, four cars were almost side by side, fighting for the lead. Fans watching the Winston 500 race at Alabama International Motor Speedway were on their feet and screaming.

In the four roaring cars were Benny Parsons, Terry Labonte, Kyle Petty, and the 1981 Grand National Champion, Darrell Waltrip. In his green-and-white Buick Regal, Waltrip studied the others. He knew he had to make his move.

He pressed down on the gas pedal and shot

around Parsons into the lead. The four cars were rushing down the backstretch. Parsons fought to get back in front, but Waltrip pressed down harder. Meanwhile, Petty and Labonte were battling for an advantage.

As a tight group the four cars thundered through turn three, then four. The roar from the fans almost drowned the roar of the cars as they streaked toward the finish line. The other three cars tried as hard as they could to get around Waltrip. The starter waited, a checkered flag in his hand.

Then he raised it and waved the flag wildly. The four cars rushed past. In the lead by only a few inches was Darrell Waltrip. It had been a typical finish of a NASCAR (National Association for Stock Car Auto Racing) race.

"If we did it all over again," said a grinning Waltrip from the victory stand, "Terry or Benny or Kyle might win. When you get down to the finish with four cars, you never know who is going to take home the bacon."

Only a month before, Waltrip had beaten the great Richard Petty by inches. Both cars had roared down the last few hundred feet of a long race side by side. Nobody knew who was going to win until the last instant.

In August, 1982, Waltrip did it again. He beat Buddy Baker by inches after 500 miles of tough racing. This time it made him the only driver ever to win the grueling Talladega 500 two times, a race also held at the Atlanta International Motor Speedway.

Yes, NASCAR racing is *very* competitive. Often the first few cars are close on the same lap at the end.

But Darrell Waltrip has always been one of the hardest-charging drivers in NASCAR. And NASCAR fans know that stock car racing is one of the toughest forms of motor racing. Not that Darrell Waltrip always wins, nor has he always been a champion. In fact, he drove for many years before he won his first race.

Born in Owensboro, Kentucky, in 1947, he always knew he wanted to be a race-car driver. So did the people of Owensboro. Some of them used to hide when young Waltrip was on the streets. He drove too fast and everybody knew it, including the local police. Waltrip even lost his driver's license because of his antics on the street.

But soon he realized that the place for speed was on a racetrack. He began driving stock cars in local events. By 1972, Darrell Waltrip had worked his way up to the top, to NASCAR. He raced in five Grand National events that year. This is the top class in stock car racing.

Stock cars in the Grand National class are racers that look like the cars on the street. But they are not. They are race cars through and

NASCAR crews actually change engines *during* a race. They set a record here with Waltrip's Gatorade racer with a complete change in only eleven minutes, thirty-six seconds. Meanwhile, Waltrip chats with his wife, Stevie.

through. They are built from the ground up to be race cars. But they still look like the passenger cars in the parking lot.

For three more years, Waltrip raced in NASCAR without a win.

"If a young driver is fast and brave and ambitious, he can make some quick progress in other types of racing," Waltrip said. "But it just isn't that way in NASCAR. When I first got into this thing, I made up my mind to ride the tide no matter what happened. For a few years it's nothing but hard work. The money's not there and the glory's not there. This NASCAR is *tough*. It's the toughest racing there is."

Finally, three years and forty races later, Waltrip won a 450-mile NASCAR race. It was the Music City 450 on his home track, Nashville International Raceway. The win was a *great* one for a local boy. But this was not a major victory. It was not a win on one of the super speedways. Then Waltrip won a race at Darlington, South Carolina, in 1977. That *was* a major victory, on one of the most famous of the super speedways.

In 1978 he won six Grand National races. Waltrip had learned his lessons well. He had learned how to win. From that moment on, he has always been one of the drivers people expect to win. And he has become a millionaire as a race-car driver.

But he has not been one of the most popular drivers.

Darrell Waltrip is one of the new breed of drivers. He doesn't mind speaking out when something happens he doesn't like. He is very aggressive on the track. This means he might push and shove a little in order to win. Other drivers push and shove too, of course, but Waltrip doesn't mind admitting it.

Tact is the ability to say something true about somebody without getting that person mad. Sometimes Waltrip just says what he has to say, without worrying about tact. Other drivers encountered this, and so did many reporters.

So there are drivers and fans who don't care all that much for the handsome, hard-driving daredevil. And it doesn't help that he just goes on with his life without making excuses. Waltrip figures he can win with or without these drivers and fans. So some of them don't care for him. Some of them even boo him.

Once at Charlotte, North Carolina, Waltrip

Darrell Waltrip (right) poses with two other famous racing drivers on a day when they competed with each other. Gordon Johncock is at left, and Mario Andretti is in the center.

had a bad wreck. It was during the 1982 World 600 race. When he crashed, some of the fans cheered.

"I really don't think they cared whether I was hurt or not," said an angry Waltrip. He had begun to try to get along with the fans. He had been making speeches and signing autographs, but nothing seemed to help. Sometimes it is fun for sports fans to have a star they can boo at. This is true in all sports. Sometimes they don't even know *why* they are booing, especially the younger fans. They do it because adults are doing it. They picked Waltrip in Grand National racing. "I think it's become a 'thing' [to boo], something people feel they *have* to do," says Waltrip.

"I've tried everything possible to get along with fans," he said after his crash. "I don't know what else to do. What I ought to do is put out a bulletin that I'll be at the Big K parking lot [a shopping center in his home town] and anybody who don't like me can show up, and we'll just duke it out. They can get out their aggression and I can vent my frustration at the same time." He wasn't smiling when he said it.

But the tide is turning. More and more fans at every race are beginning to *cheer* Darrell Waltrip. They are seeing that he is truly one of the top stars in NASCAR. In fact, in 1981 he became the champion. He had lost the championship in 1979 by only 11 points (out of a possible 10,000). He'd lost it to the great "King" Richard Petty. He lost to Dale Earnhardt in 1980, though he won five races and placed in the top five sixteen times. Finally, in 1981, he was the Grand National Champion.

The top championship wasn't all he won in 1981. He earned the Jerry Titus Memorial Award from the American Auto Racing Writers and Broadcasters Association. It is that group's top award. Waltrip got more votes from these experts than any other driver in all of racing. He became the first stock car driver ever to win this honor.

For the third year in a row he was voted onto that same group's All America team of drivers.

Waltrip also won the Olsonite Driver of the Year award for the second time. This is a very important award, since it means he was picked as the top racing driver of the year by still another group of auto racing experts, journalists, sponsors, and others who know the sport well.

Waltrip won an amazing twelve races out of thirty in 1981. He placed high in many others. He had become the top winning driver in all of NASCAR. Driving his now-famous Mountain Dew Buick (his pit crew is called the "Dew Crew"), Waltrip charged on in 1982, winning or threatening in every race.

Are drivers like Waltrip, Petty, Parsons, and

In a frenzy of speed and thunder that shakes the camera, Waltrip roars past on his way to win in the Mountain Dew Buick.

others in other types of racing really athletes? The question has been asked many times. Just how tough is it, really, to drive a race car?

Waltrip won the Nashville 420 in 1981. The day was hot and humid. It was almost suffocating. Inside a stock car, the temperature was even hotter. Many fans fainted from the heat. Drivers were suffering. Finally the rough race ended.

In Victory Circle, Waltrip passed out. He had a huge blister on his right foot from engine heat. His right leg was cramping badly. His stomach was aching. His driving uniform was soaked through with perspiration.

Lying on the press room floor he said, "This should put an end to the question as to whether race-car drivers are athletes." Race-car drivers must be in excellent physical condition — as Waltrip is — to stand the strain of driving. Sometimes, however, even fine condition isn't enough. Most race-car drivers are athletes. They *must* be.

Grand National racing is also very scientific. The race cars are expensive. They are handmade and the engines are built with great care and precision. Each car has many safety devices to protect the driver, such as roll cages and on-board fire extinguishers. Each car has one or more radios to keep the driver aware of what is happening. Many crews listen in on other drivers' frequencies so they can tell their own driver of any problems. They even listen in on the plans of the other teams.

"It's been going on a long time," says the outspoken Waltrip. "It's no big deal. Everybody does it. At least all the top teams."

Even with radio contact with drivers, mistakes are made. Once, at Pocono Raceway, Darrell Waltrip was heading for Victory Circle after the Pocono 500-mile stock car race. But when he got there, Cale Yarborough was already accepting the trophy.

Disappointed but still certain he'd won, Waltrip waited outside the celebration. His wife stood by his side trying to cheer him up. She was also sure he had won the tough race.

Sure enough, NASCAR officials finally asked Yarborough to leave and Waltrip to come in. It is very difficult to keep track of a race with many cars. There are many pit stops and accidents, and cars can get mixed up. Sometimes sorting it out takes a few minutes. In that race, Yarborough and Waltrip had flashed across the finish line almost side by side. Yarborough was slightly ahead. Actually he was almost one full lap *behind,* but he and his crew didn't know that. Waltrip did.

Darrell Waltrip runs many races during the year. He races all thirty of the NASCAR Grand National races. He also races in ten to fifteen late-model stock car races.

A dejected Waltrip waits outside victory lane with his
wife while officials decide who won. He did.

"A race driver is a lot like a horse," he told Shav Glick of the *Los Angeles Times*. "If you don't use him he gets lazy. The more you race, the more you learn, too. You'd be surprised how little things I pick up driving late-model races help in the Grand Nationals."

One of the most exciting races of all to Waltrip is the Busch Clash. This is a short (fifty miles) flat-out high-speed rush among all the fastest drivers of the year before. It is the first race of every new season for the Grand National stock

There's no doubt about this victory. Waltrip sprays champagne on the trophy girl and his car owner, Junior Johnson.

cars. If you won a pole position (the fastest car in qualifying for any race) then you can race in the Busch Clash at Daytona International Speedway in February.

Darrell Waltrip has the best record of all the top drivers in this very difficult race. He has won it, and he always places high in it. He has won more money than anybody else in the Busch Clash.

By 1982, thirty-five-year-old Darrell Waltrip had become a regular winner. He had won dozens of races. He holds many, many racing speed records. Although he is very aggressive on the track, he is outgoing and friendly in the pits. There are very few boos anymore for Waltrip.

What does the future hold for him? He is young, and he is one of the best. He has a single driving ambition. He is at the top, and he wants to *stay* there.

Darrell Waltrip wants to win the NASCAR Grand National Championship again . . . and again . . . and again.

Rick Mears

FIVE

RICK MEARS

The 1981 Indy Speedway race thundered out on the track. The young driver had pulled into his pit seconds ago. He was doing well. But he needed fuel. Normally a fuel stop takes only a few seconds at the Indy 500. Everybody works very quickly so that the car can get back into the race.

Rick Mears sat in the cockpit of his sleek racer as crewmen added fuel. He had won the Indy race in 1979 and he wanted to win it again. His car was running well. He felt good as he sat there waiting.

Then something went wrong. The fuel hose didn't close off as it was unhooked from the race car. Methanol, the fuel used in Indy cars, sprayed all over the place. It sprayed around the pit and onto the crewmen. It sprayed into the cockpit of the racer.

Mears felt the dangerous fuel splash across his face inside his opened helmet. It soaked the chest of his driving uniform. "I knew I was in trouble," he recalled later.

Quickly he tried to unsnap his seat belts. He knew the fuel would ignite the instant it hit something hot. Around a race car, *everything* is hot. Then he felt his chest getting warmer and warmer. He knew his fire-resistant suit was burning. He had only a few seconds left.

He didn't know that his pit and car were burning wildly. He didn't know that one of his crewmen was being seriously burned. He didn't know that his wife had fallen from the eight-foot-high timing stand to get away from the fire.

He only knew that *he* was on fire. His face was burning. He must not breathe. If he did, the fire would go into his lungs. He had been trained to hold his breath in a fire. He struggled to get out of the burning car.

Worse yet, nobody knew he was on fire. Methanol burns without visible flames. Firemen were trying to put out the fire around the car. They didn't realize the driver was burning.

Mears finally managed to leap from the car and

run to a fireman. The fireman still didn't know the driver was on fire. Mears grabbed a fire extinguisher and aimed it at his face. He was in terrible pain by then, and still he did not dare breathe.

Mears' father was in the pit. He saw that his son was in serious trouble. As the fireman ran from the flames, Mears' father ran forward and grabbed another extinguisher. Ignoring the flames, he blasted the chemicals over his son. Finally the fire went out and Mears could take a breath. His face was seriously burned. Of course he was out of the race.

But eventually Rick Mears recovered. He had plastic surgery on his nose to replace the tip that had been burned away. Soon he was back racing again, and winning again.

Motor racing is always a dangerous sport. Unexpected things happen. They happen to drivers who never win, and they happen to champions like Rick Mears. But racing is in the blood of Rick Mears and his family. His father was a racer in Wichita, Kansas.

The story of Rick Mears in racing is more like a Hollywood movie than real life. He climbed to the top very fast. He became a winner in only his second race at the famous Indianapolis Speedway. He has continued on as a champion, winning the National Driving Championship in 1979, 1981, and again in 1982.

Did the Indy pit fire hurt his skill as a driver?

Mears missed the next race because he was in the hospital. But with bandages still on his face he came back to race in the next event only a few weeks later, a twin race at Atlanta. He won *both races* against the top drivers in Indy car racing. There was no doubt that Rick Mears was back. He went on to win four of the last six Indy car

In 1983, Rick Mears' latest car was a bright yellow Pennzoil Special, owned by Roger Penske.

races that year. He seemed to be even better than before, if that was possible.

Mears is a handsome driver who is very popular with racing fans. He is a fine public speaker and makes many speeches for his sponsors. He has never allowed his fame to go to his head.

In his hometown of Bakersfield, California, and in most other racing cities, he is often stopped on the street. Fans just want to talk to him or get his autograph. He never refuses, even if he is in a hurry. He remembers when he was trying very hard to get started in championship racing. He

At a celebrity race, Mears meets his co-driver, actor James Brolin. The team won the race.

feels the fans are responsible for his being where he is. He will always be nice to them.

Mears' mother and father used to take him and his older brother, Roger, for motorcycle rides. Both parents loved motorcycle riding. So both boys developed a love for bikes. Both became riders, and soon Rick wanted to race motorcycles. He won over sixty trophies between the ages of sixteen and eighteen.

But Mears' mother was worried. So Mears' father built a dune-buggy-type racer, and the boys became interested in off-road racing. Soon both were champions in this type of racing.

Roger Mears is still a champion off-road racer. But he is moving into Indy-type racing, just as his younger brother did. Rick, meanwhile, decided to race some formula cars in road races. These were amateur events sanctioned by the SCCA, the Sports Car Club of America. Mears chose Formula Vee cars to start with. These are fast racers powered by Volkswagen engines. It is a class where many other young drivers have started, including several who went on to become World Driving Champions. From Formula Vee Mears moved to Super Vee, a faster class. Then to Formula 5000, an even faster class of racer.

During this time he also won the famous Pikes Peak Hill Climb.

Finally he got his big break. He got a chance to drive Championship (Indy-type) cars. These are the fastest oval-track racers of all. His big chance came when he met Roger Penske, a man who runs one of the best racing teams. Penske was looking for a new driver to team with Bobby Unser and Mario Andretti. What a fine chance for a young driver! He wouldn't be the number one driver on the team, but it would be a great opportunity to learn in the best cars and from the most expert drivers.

Mears jumped at the job when Penske offered it. He considers it the greatest thing to happen to him in racing.

Racing drivers have a millionaire's club. These are the drivers who have earned more than one million dollars in their career. Dale Earnhardt became the driver who got into the club fastest. It took him only seventy-six stock car races to earn one million dollars.

Then along came Rick Mears. He got into the club after only fifty-eight races. He got into the club faster than any of the other super-champion drivers, including A. J. Foyt, Richard Petty, Mario Andretti, Gordon Johncock, or either of the Unser brothers, Bobby and Al.

Mears is known as a "finisher" in big-time auto racing. He can finish a race in a car that another driver might not be able to keep going. He knows how to keep a car running even if it has a mechanical problem. At the end of 1981, Mears had finished an amazing 53 percent of his races in the *top four*. He had finished 85 percent in the top ten. Nobody has ever come close to that record of finishing races.

The crew swarms around Mears' car during a pit stop.

Twenty-nine-year-old Rick Mears was the champion for the second time in spite of his fire at the Indianapolis Speedway. He was the best Indy car driver of all. Yet he had never won a race at the one-mile Phoenix, Arizona, track. He had tried seven times.

Roger Penske was Mears' car owner. Penske was a winner as a driver and a winner as an owner. His cars were said to be the best by most drivers. Penske had ideas that always made his cars faster. Penske drivers always seemed to win the big races. Yet Roger Penske had never won at Phoenix. In nineteen tries, his cars had never won.

The first race of the new 1982 season was to be held at Phoenix. Both Mears and Penske knew it would be great to start the season with a victory. But the odds were against them. Nobody expected them to win at their "bad luck" track. Instead, Mears led almost all the way and won the race easily. The jinx had been broken.

Rick Mears' first great triumph had come at the Indianapolis Speedway in 1979. It was only his second year at the famous Brickyard. The first year he had placed twenty-third after having engine problems. But that wasn't the whole story for 1978. He had qualified on the *front row* for the start. He was the third fastest car in the field, an amazing feat for a brand-new driver.

Later he was voted "Co-Rookie of the Year" with driver Larry Rice, who also did a fine job in the race.

There was no stopping the young driving star in 1979. He qualified "on the pole" at Indy, the fastest car in the race. At the end of the race, he was fourteen seconds ahead of A. J. Foyt. To a great thunder of applause from more than a quarter million spectators, he took the checkered flag.

That same year he won the Jerry Titus Memorial Award from the American Auto Racing Writers and Broadcasters Association. This meant he had been voted the best driver in racing by a group of experts.

Mears had moved up fast in racing, but it had been a hobby for him for many years before. "Everything I ever raced was just because I loved racing," he said. "I never did anything in any type of racing trying to better my career. I didn't even think of career. This was my hobby. I did it because I loved it and enjoyed doing it."

Here's Rick Mears in victory lane at the biggest win of his life, the Indianapolis 500 in 1979.

Still, everything worked out just right for Mears. He moved to the top faster than any other driver.

"The only goal I have ever set is to equal or do better than I did at that before," he said. "Do that, and you'll be all right."

One of Mears' most exciting races was at Michigan International Speedway in 1981. His Indianapolis burns were still pink and sore, but that didn't stop him. He was battling with Mario Andretti late in the 150-mile race. He needed the victory to get the 1981 National Championship. Going into the last lap, Andretti was a car length ahead.

Through turn one the cars were side by side. Then the power of Andretti's STP Oil Treatment Special won out, and Mario pulled ahead down the backstretch. Rick Mears knew he had the advantage in the turns, though.

"I could run under Mario on both ends of the track," he explained later. "But I knew if I did it in turn one or two, he would probably get me back before I got to the finish line. So I just tried to stay as close to him as I could, and when we went into turn three I just ran in without lifting [off the gas]. I turned in under him and didn't lift and ran the car almost down on the safety apron trying to shorten the corner up as much as I could."

So the two cars, Andretti's and Mears' familiar Gould Charge Penske PC-9B Cosworth, battled into the final straightaway.

"He had a little bit more than me on the straightaways, so I knew I had to get as much as possible off the corner. I ran it down real tight to get a little bit more drive on him, and it paid off," Mears explained.

With thousands of fans screaming for the two popular drivers, Mears inched ahead. He was ahead by less than one-half car length as the checkered flag snapped down.

"Sorry about that," a grinning Mears said to Andretti in Victory Circle. Both drivers shook hands as Andretti grinned back.

Mears was involved in the closest finish ever at the Indianapolis Motor Speedway at the end of the 1982 500-mile race. Few fans will forget Mears' dramatic charge in the final ten laps of that race. He tried with all his skill to catch Gordon Johncock. He was behind by only a tenth of a second at the end. Most experts agree that he needed one more lap. But the Indy race is 200 laps, not 201.

Mears has had some crazy wins. In the 1978 Milwaukee Rex Mays 150, he was leading by a good margin. But then his car ran out of gas with four laps to go. So he turned down the boost (a power adjustment that also uses extra gas) and began to nurse his racer toward the finish. He looked like a turnpike driver trying to make it to the next service exit. Slower and slower went the Mears racer as he used the very last of the fuel. He even swerved from side to side to slosh any remaining fuel into the lines.

He crossed the finish line slowly but still two seconds ahead of a hard-charging Johnny Rutherford.

Does an Indy champion ever feel fear? Mears was asked the question.

"You're running 200 miles per hour, a foot or so from the wall, and you could be saying to yourself

Mears leads this line of Indy cars.

'if a tire blew, it would be yesterday.' But if you start thinking about it, pretty soon you're going to start slowing down.

"So, I just don't think about it."

Mears is the only driver since the great A. J. Foyt to be compared to Foyt. Foyt himself says that Mears could be the "Foyt of the eighties."

Rick Mears is proving the truth of that prediction. He is often a winner, and he is always an exciting driver to watch.

Alan Jones

SIX

ALAN JONES

The start of a Formula 1 Grand Prix race is one of the most exciting moments in all of sports. The start of the Long Beach (California) Grand Prix has proven to be one of the most exciting in all of Grand Prix racing.

One driver has mastered Grand Prix starts and Long Beach starts to become the World Driving Champion. His name is Alan Jones.

Picture this: A couple of dozen of the finest racing machines in the world are lined up on the grid. They are all the colors of the rainbow. Crowds mill about them. Celebrities — musicians, actors, famous people from many countries — rubberneck and photograph the cars. Various languages flow among spectators and drivers and crews. Reporters and news photographers battle for position for last-minute material. Meanwhile, drivers are being strapped into their cars. They are lying down, almost flat on their backs.

Their eyes flick about the cockpit as they check last-minute details with their mechanics.

Then the engines start and howl with power. Quickly the track clears of people.

Slowly, very slowly, the cars pull away from their "false grid" and make a tour of the track. They are in their starting order. Fans all around the twisting, turning track wave and cheer them on as they rumble by. Some of the drivers wave back. Some nod. Others are icy calm as they idle by, staring straight ahead. All are preparing for what is to come.

In a group they approach the true grid where marks on the track show each car where to stop. All the powerful cars are quickly in position. Up ahead, where everybody can see him, is the flagman. He indicates that only one minute remains before the start.

The drivers are now tense. Gone is the joking and laughing of moments before. Their hands grip the tiny steering wheels and their feet wait poised over clutch, brake, and gas pedals. Although everybody expects the signal, it is still a surprise when it comes.

A great green flag rises and falls. A light flashes from red to green at the same instant.

Every single engine thunders with a burst of power and tires squeal as each tries to bite into the track surface. Weaving and sliding about, each car fights for a place as the entire pack screams away. It is a very dangerous moment. Some have not lived through it.

Until recently at Long Beach, an even more dangerous moment was ahead. For a number of years, until the track was changed, the cars started at the top of the long backstretch. This gave them nearly a mile to get up their speed, all in a bunch.

Then came a hard right *hairpin* turn.

Each year at the start the cars would roar away, going faster and faster. Then, as they approached the hairpin, they would squeal and slide, trying to slow down and fall into a single line. Each year some did not make it.

Cars would fly over each other, or bounce off each other, or spin out. Some would fly down a nearby escape road, unable to manage the turn. The place was a wild and dangerous one for every driver.

Most cars, however, made it through to go on and fight out the race.

Alan Jones made it through every time — at Long Beach and at most other Grand Prix tracks

There is nothing like the start of a Grand Prix Formula 1 race. Sometimes cars jump completely over other cars.

around the world. At one track he did a complete 360-degree spin. Missing the walls and other cars, he went on without losing his position.

Grand Prix racing, called Formula 1 racing, is "world class" motor racing. There are tracks in many different countries. The cars and crews and drivers go from country to country to race.

Alan Jones became the World Driving Champion in Formula 1 racing. This means he is the top driver in what many fans consider to be the top form of racing in the world. Jones' career on the way to becoming the champion is more like one in a story than real life. It seems almost exactly what you might think a racing driver's career should be.

Jones' father was a famous racing driver in Australia. He was Stan Jones, winner of the 1952 New Zealand Grand Prix and known to every racing fan of that era. In Australia, Jones' home country, Stan Jones was a sports idol. It seemed only natural that Stan Jones' son, Alan, would follow in his famous father's footsteps. And he did.

As a teen-ager, Alan Jones became a champion in racing karts. Karts are flat little buzz bombs

Jones, and many other drivers, got their start in karts like these at the Long Beach Grand Prix.

where the driver actually does lie flat on his back to race. From the little, tiny-wheeled racers, Jones fought his way all the way to the world championship.

From his days as a kart racer to his days on Formula 1 victory stands around the world, Alan Jones never changed. He remained a friendly, witty, outgoing man, with a good word for everybody. He remained happy and popular among racing fans in many different countries. He never turned away a request for a word or two with a fan and he always spoke to everybody in a very straightforward way.

But it wasn't easy for Jones. He had to fight his

way to the top as his father had done before him. Sure, you get some breaks if you are the son of a famous father, but you still have to sit in the cockpit and drive the car. Certain sons of driver star fathers are doing it today: The Unser boys, Michael Andretti, and others. They may have gotten a better car because of their name, but they still have to drive it on the track.

That is where the challenge is — and the danger.

So it wasn't easy for Alan Jones. In fact, his father put him to work as a salesman even after he became a race driver. Jones was racing in his own Cooper-Climax as well as a Formula 2 racer then. Both of these cars are on the ladder of auto racing, but they are not near the top.

Then Alan Jones dropped out for a year. Perhaps he was discouraged. Maybe he felt a responsibility to his wife. Possibly he didn't think he had a future in driving. He took various jobs. Once he sold used motor homes outside the lodging house his wife managed.

Round-faced and cherubic looking, Jones did not seem to fit the picture of a dashing Grand Prix driver. But that was always what he dreamed of becoming. To Alan Jones and hundreds of other young drivers around the world, Grand Prix was the top. These were the best cars and drivers. This was the most dramatic and exciting life.

These drivers dined with kings and queens and stayed in the very best hotels. They had fancy cars and airplanes and were held in high esteem by all racing fans. These drivers lived high and defied death on racing weekends. If they survived, they were often millionaires who retired young to enjoy life. They were the matadors of motor racing.

And Alan Jones wanted to be one.

So he moved to England in 1969. He settled into a serious effort in Formula 3 racing at first in his own car. By 1971 he was one of the top drivers on factory teams in this class. This means he was driving somebody else's car, for pay.

Alan Jones was around the fringes of Formula 1. He drove in Formula Atlantic, then Formula 5000, cars similar to Formula 1. He continued to polish his great natural skill and talent. He began to win more and more often. Occasionally he would get hired by a Formula 1 team for a race or two. He was being seen.

He was hired by the great Graham Hill, a former Formula 1 driver with a keen eye for talent. Then, in a few weeks, the Shadow team hired him to fill in when one of their drivers, Tom Pryce, was killed. The Shadow team was another well-known Formula 1 team. Finally, in 1977, what everybody expected, happened.

In a brilliant drive in a terrible rainstorm, Alan Jones won a Formula 1 race, the Austrian Grand Prix. In that tough race Jones gave the Shadow team their only Grand Prix victory. As he stood in the mist and rain on the victory stand and watched the Australian flag go up a flagpole he knew he was where he wanted to be. In the background a band was playing "Advance Australia Fair." These are the customs in Formula 1 Grand Prix racing. The national flag and anthem of the winning driver is a part of victory ceremonies. The moving ceremony has brought many tough drivers and mechanics to tears.

At the end of 1977, Jones moved over to the Frank Williams Saudia team. It was the break he had been waiting for.

Auto racing teams are sponsored by many different products. Some of the products are not even connected with cars. Teams have been

Alan Jones resembles a spaceman as he prepares for a race. The tube going into his helmet carries the radio connection with his pit crew.

sponsored by blue jeans companies, camera companies, perfume companies, and beer companies. The richer the company, the better off the team. Grand Prix racing takes a *lot* of money. Some sponsors put more money into a team than other sponsors. The Williams team had an unusual sponsor indeed. And a *rich* one.

"The team should be called the Saudi People's Racing Team," said Frank Williams, the team owner. "It really represents the whole country." The team had picked up a group of Arabian companies as sponsors. The cars were painted white, green, and gold, the royal Arabian colors. On the sides were lettered strange names like *Albilad, TAG, Dallah Avco,* and *Saudia.*

Millions of dollars in sponsorship money was pouring into the Williams team. The team began to win races with Alan Jones at the wheel. Jones was also enjoying the attention of the new sponsors. However, the Arabs maintained a low profile around the Grand Prix tracks.

"I would like to see four or five sheiks in robes, riding camels or carrying falcons on their arms, hanging around our pits," said Jones, with a grin. "We'd love the attention they would bring, but they don't operate that way. They dress just like Europeans or Americans — with expensive tastes, though."

In 1980 the Williams team prepared for the Canadian Grand Prix. The world championship is won on a basis of points earned by the driver. A certain number of points are awarded for high finishes in each race throughout the year. The season was nearing an end, with only one more race after Canada. But Jones might not need that last race. He had enough points so that if he won the race in Canada, no other driver could beat him for the World Driving Championship.

Fans in Montreal packed into the grandstands for the exciting race. At the start, before the field even reached the first turn, there was a terrible accident. Jones and the second-place driver in the points standings, Nelson Piquet, bumped together. It happened during their frantic effort to get into the turn first. The bumping sent Piquet spinning sideways, and instantly the crowded track was full of spinning cars. Mario Andretti's car flew into the air and began to turn over. But to Andretti's great luck, another spinning car struck him and flipped him right-side-up *in the air*. He landed on his wheels and later returned to the race.

The cars of Jean-Pierre Jarier, Derek Daly, Keke Rosberg, Gilles Villeneuve, and Jochen Mass all crashed back and fourth. It was a million dollar destruction derby.

Grand Prix cars are said to be the most perfect machines humans can make. Jones leads the way around a turn on a Grand Prix track.

Alan Jones, fighting for the lead and the championship, streaked away. He left the carnage far behind. There was a huge black tire mark on the side of his car. Driver after driver tried to catch him, but it was no use. If anyone did manage to pass him, he stayed right behind them *very* close until they made a mistake ... or until their engine blew apart from the strain. When the checkered flag fell, the white-and-green Saudia car was in the lead.

Alan Jones had won the race — and the World Driving Championship.

On the victory stand he grinned. "It's something I've dreamed about since I was eight," he said. "I've been trying so hard, and the team has been trying so hard, and it has been such a struggle that my feelings now are more of relief than elation. It'll probably come to me in the shower and I'll start jumping up and down."

From then on Alan Jones was the driver to beat. He was the champion. At every track, photographers followed him and questioned him about the races. He seemed to enjoy the attention.

Alan Jones and the Saudia/Williams team came roaring back in 1981. Nobody paid much attention to the fact that Jones and his wife had sold their home in Long Beach, California. It was a fine home, overlooking the track for the Long Beach Grand Prix. Quietly, Jones had bought a 1,600 acre cattle-and-horse ranch in Australia.

On the track he was as fast as ever, as skilled as ever. On victory stands he was as friendly as ever. He opened the 1981 season by winning the difficult Long Beach Grand Prix. American fans cheered him. He had lived in the United States, and they considered him one of them.

In Brazil he finished second behind his Williams teammate, Carlos Reutemann. They cheered the champion in South America. They cheered in Belgium, France, Monaco, Spain, England, Germany, Austria, Holland, Italy, and Canada as Jones charged through the season in race after race. In every race he was a threat, always battling near the front or for the lead.

Around a tight corner at the Long Beach Grand Prix goes Alan Jones on his way to victory. This is one of the very few Grand Prix races held on city streets.

Then the season drew to an end. There was one race left: the brand-new Caesars Palace Grand Prix in Las Vegas, Nevada. Jones had an announcement for the press. Those who had been following the season and the champion closely had a good idea of what he was going to say, but the fans were stunned. This, he said quietly, would be his last Grand Prix. The champion was going to retire.

When the race was over, it was Alan Jones on

This is a shot of Las Vegas, specifically Caesars Palace, with the track outlined in white on the vast Caesars parking lot. Jones won the first race on this track.

CAESARS PALACE
GRAND PRIX RACETRACK LAYOUT

the victory stand. In the setting sun, he repeated his vow to quit. He'd done it all. He'd won more than his share of very dangerous, very demanding races. He'd been the world champion. He'd survived. He was wealthy. Now he wanted to go home to his farm with his wife and son. And he did.

"We have everything on the farm we need," he said. "We can grow all the food we need to eat." He seemed contented in retirement after years of thrilling racing.

But not for long.

Others have come back from retirement. Some of them have come back and won again. Some have died on the racetrack after coming back. Always they came back because they couldn't resist the call to further adventures.

Alan Jones came back in only one year. He is as friendly and hard-driving as ever. Nobody knows what his future will be. But fans will always compare the new crop of fresh and eager young drivers with the standard set by veteran Alan Jones.

INDEX

Page numbers in *italics* refer to captions.